THE HISTORY OF HIP HOP

VOLUME 3

ERIC REESE

CONTENTS

Hip-hop is the streets. Hip-hop is a couple of elements that it comes from back in the days... that feel of music with urgency that speaks to you. It speaks to your livelihood and it's not compromised. It's blunt. It's raw, straight off the street - from the beat to the voice to the words.

NAS

INTRODUCTION

These days, hip hop surrounds us really everywhere, whether it is on TV in the form of movies, music shows, or commercials, on the radio, or just in the streets, where various public places are aged-tagged, or when groups of young people make shows by breaking or rapping in front of randomly passing people in order to make some money, have fun and show what they can do. Shortly, nearly everyone has a certain idea about what is hip hop. It is such a complex area that includes music, dance, art such as graffiti, fashion, and many other fields which are connected with it, which still needs to be introduced and therefore the aim of this book is to make the further acquaintance of hip hop not only as a musical style, but as a whole phenomenon of hip hop culture which has been spreading among youth especially through the media across the whole world.

Since its creation, Hip Hop has had a cultural impact on youth all around the world. The youth specifically because the music, for many, is a reflection of their lives and is told in a way they can easily understand. Beginning in the South Bronx of New York in November of 1974, Hip Hop consisted mainly of DJing, breaking (break dancing), graffiti, and rapping. However, it is much more than just a kind of music. Many believe that the genre can be seen as a way of life, given that it also has brought about new ways of dressing, expression, and its unique outlooks on cultural, political, economical and intellectual factors in society.

1 HIP HOP AT A GLANCE

There are several mistakes that circulate among people. For example, a lot of people think hip hop is only a musical style and that hip hop and rap is the same thing. Therefore, I would like to explain some terms that are concerned with hip hop at the beginning of this essay.

Firstly, hip hop is not only a musical style, it includes a large number of areas, and music is just one of them. It is quite difficult to define hip hop because of its complexity, but there are several definitions of this phenomenon such as a US pop culture movement originating in the 1980s comprising rap music, graffiti and break dancing" or a popular urban youth culture, closely associated with rap music and with the style and fashions of African-American inner-city residents, the most precious definition of hip hop can be found in Martin Fiedler's Hip hop Forever: "Hip hop is a life-style with a developed and colorful culture, its language, and fashion style, specific kind of music and thinking, which is constantly developing."

Another interesting opinion of what hip hop is, belongs to DJ and MC TC Izlam, who claims: "Hip hop is just a way of thinking, state of mind. To be a hip-hopper means to think freely." The second mistake that hip hop and rap can be used synonymously is also very common among people who do not understand this issue. From the definitions that are mentioned above is clear what hip hop means. Rap is "a rhythmic mono-logue with musical backing, "which means that it's just a lexical part of hip hop music which is just one of the several parts of whole hip hop culture.

The name "Hip Hop" is said to have been coined by Keith "Cowboy" Wiggins. Wiggins was a member of Grandmaster Flash and the Furious Five, a Hip-Hip group formed in 1978 in the South Bronx. They were a large part of the genre's earliest pioneers. Other artists signifying the beginning of Hip Hop include The Sugar Hill Gang. Signed by Sylvia Robinson, they have been recognized as the first popular rap group. Their song, "Rapper's Delight," is still popular today.

The first female group to release a Hip Hop single was known as The Sequence, releasing "Funk You Up" in 1979 while the first female solo artist to do so was Lady B in the same year.

2 REVIEW OF THE ELEMENTS OF HIP HOP

We wrote on this topic in our second volume of the History of Hip Hop and is listing again to give background to those who are new to the series.

Hip hop culture contains four essential elements: DJing, MCing, graffiti art and b-boying. DJing and MCing symbolize a musical part, b-boying stands for a dance component, and graffiti represents a visual art constituent of this culture. Of course, these four elements did not originate at the same time, but their combination enabled hip hop to come into existence.

DJing

DJing is a fundamental means to produce hip hop music. The DJ is the abbreviation for the phrase 'disc jockey' – a person, who plays recorded, not live, music or sound for an audience. The very first disc jockeys were radio DJs, who played the music to radio listeners and in the 1950s, DJs started to perform "live" at various parties. Americans were always used to dancing at a bar to music from a jukebox, but paying for a DJ not playing "live" music was not very common.

In 1973, DJ Kool Herc took two turntables, which he connected to a mixer and he laid two identical records on the turntables. The mixer helps DJ in the smooth transition of sound from one turntable to the second one. Kool Herc played a break of one record and the same break of the second record, which he could easily repeat. This method is known as "mixing breaks"6 or "creating breakbeats"7. Herc played the music for an audience of dancers who are known as b-boys, or break boys, and b-girls or break girls. Under the influence of DJ Kool Herc, some of the b-boys such as Grandmixer DXT and Kurtis Blow became DJs too. Herc contributed to the development of DJing by creating a huge mobile sound system, because he knew how to connect more speakers and generate more electrical power to be able to make a louder sound. Another innovative DJ was Grandmaster Flash, who brought to perfection the Herc's way of mixing two records. He developed a theory called a "quick mix theory," which is based upon marking records and using a headset to be able to hear how is the second record combined with the first one before the audience can hear it via the loudspeaker and make a fluent transition from one record to the other.

Grand Wizard Theodore, a pupil of Grandmaster Flash, accidentally created a technique of DJing called "scratching." One day of the year 1975, when he was improving his DJing skills at home, his mother told him to turn down the volume. Because he did not hear it, she entered his room and he tried to stop the music by laying his hand on the playing record to stop its spinning. By moving it back and forward to keep the record quiet and be able to listen to his mother's words, he noted that this movement creates a unique sound. It is necessary to mention that this technique is commonly used by DJs up to this day.

In the mid-1990s came to the rise of the turntablism movement, which caused the DJing became again one of the essential elements of Hip Hop. It was a new generation of DJs, who wanted to regain the dominant role of the DJ in the music and make the turntable to be a musical instrument again. The advances in technology in the twenty-first century moved DJing to the next level. Because of digital technology, DJs are allowed to play music through digital music files saved in notebooks or the use of CD players. These technological advances allow almost everyone to become a DJ because DJs do not need to have a wide collection of records anymore, which require a lot of space and also can be expensive.

Over time, DJs started to use microphones and talk to their audiences to keep them interested and MCs took the role later.

M Cing

MCing is often used as a synonym for rapping, but it is just one part of what an MC does. The MC is the acronym of the phrase 'master of ceremonies and over time, the title MC began to be used as an abbreviation for phrases such as 'microphone controller' or 'microphone checker'. The role of MC is the assistance to DJ in keeping the audience excited and entertained and encouraging b-boys and b-girls to dance. To be an MC provided an opportunity to express one's feelings and opinions of society and the environment in which one lives. Coke La Rock, who cooperated with DJ Kool Herc, was the first significant hip hop MC. In the mid-1970s, MCs were not only helpers of DJs, but they became their partners. From the combination of DJ and MC evolved a large number of groups. The advances in technology changed the relationship between DJ and MC. Thanks to the digital audiotape and the cassette, MCs of the 1980s were able to perform without the presence of DJs because they could play recorded music through these cassettes and tapes. The value of MCs also rose in the eyes of record labels, who sought out talented MCs such as KRS-One, Kurtis Blow, Queen Latifah or Rakim. Thanks to them, MCs became hip hop super-stars and icons of popular culture. The growing impor-tance of MCs caused that they gained the success and grabbed all the money.No wonder that MCs became so significant in hip hop culture when they are supposed to have several skills to be able to fulfill their roles. MCs have a high degree of originality and versatility; attain a high level of mastery over substance, flow, and 'battle skills'; have a significant social impact, and possess outstanding live performance abilities."

B -boying

B-boying is a kind of street dance and it is often called 'breakdancing' or 'breaking'. It was inspired by dance elements of other dance styles that already existed, but breakers except that they adapt old moves also invent a large number of new ones. It is a very diffi-cult kind of dance and keeping balance and being flexible play an important role when doing the breaking. History of b-boying goes back to the 1970s when each gang contained a crew of dancers. The old-school rap historians claim that "the first break dancers were... street gang members who danced upright."10 These dancers were predominantly African American and they took breaking only as a way of dancing. The question is, whether breaking would have still existed if Hispanic teenagers had not become excited about it. It was the Hispanics, who brought competitiveness into b-boying. Crews of b-boys and b-girls dared other breakers to meet them at a specific place, where they created a circle in which pairs of dancers alternate in dancing, till one of the dance crews are recognized as the winning one. In 1982, b-boying/b-girling got to the mainstream by performing of Rock Steady Crew on ABC News, where they battled against the Dynamic Rockers. Among the fundamental techniques of b-boying belong toprock, uprock, downrock, power moves, and freeze.

Other Elements

Over time, as hip hop was rising and spreading, another element began to enter the hip hop culture. In the 1980s, Afrika Bambaataa, one of the excellent DJs, tried to enforce a fifth element that was called "Knowledge, Culture and Overstanding. It consisted of comprehending the principles laid by the hip hop pioneers and the conceptual history of the preceding elements. The term "overstanding" contained a positivist ideology taken from Rastafarianism, which emphasized a superior positive power, not on the negative one. Others wanted "beatboxing," which is vocal percussion imitating various musical sounds and instruments, to be the fifth element, but it continues to be an underground phenomenon within hip hop culture. In the 1980s, as hip hop became national music, the people listening to this kind of music needed to identify with it by selecting a particular kind of clothes. Clothing companies and shoe manufacturers such as Adidas, Nike, and Timberland gave them this opportunity. This specific clothing includes pieces such as saggy pants, oversized T-shirts, hooded coats and sweatshirts, and hip hop caps. Because hip hop culture arose and evolved on the street, a particular language style is an integral part of it. It is the slang, because of which hip hop has often been criticized, but as hip hop became mainstream, a lot of expressions got into wider society and also current dictionaries. For example in the Oxford English Dictionary, we can find a definition of the noun and the adjective bling bling, which sounds:

"denoting expensive, ostentatious clothing or jewelry, or the style or materialistic attitudes associated with them." It is important to mention that the four basic elements did not arise along with hip hop. They existed independently of it, but their combination enabled the birth of this culture.

3 ELEMENTS OF B-BOYING

T oprock

Toward the beginning of b-boying, break-dance was about the toprock. It is the most basic procedure, which incorporates a wide range of moves done in a standing position. Toprock is normally the initial step of a dancer, who at that point continues going downwards. A b-boy historian called Jorge "Pop-master Fabel" Pabon says about the beginnings of breaking: "It was all carefully top-shaking, intriguing drops to get down to the floor, incredible blitz-speed foot-work. It was entirely unpredictable. Bouncing around, rotating, turning, turns, front-clears, you know? What's more, aggressive, extremely aggressive, to the point that I thought it was a gang dance at first."

. . .

Uprock

This technique arose before b-boying itself, just to be more specific, it came into existence in Brooklyn during the 1960s. When breakers were doing uprock, "rivals lined up across each other, and went head-to-head – making as if they were jigging, stabbing, battering each other."The uprock style requires two rival breakers or crews who dance toprock alternatively whole time the song is playing. It looks like the dancers were fighting with each other, but there is not any physical contact allowed in this dance. The winning dancer or crew is the one that shows better and faster dance elements and combinations.

Downrock

The downrock is a dance technique which is also called "footwork". The pioneer of this style was the crew called Rock Steady Crew, which was established in the South Bronx in 1977. It describes all kinds of movements which are performed on the floor and the emphasis is put especially on feet, but hands are commonly used to support the dancer. The 6-step is the basic move of the downrock and it simply reminds of walking in a circle on the floor with one hand touching the ground. Except for the use of feet and hands, the legs and knees can be also involved in performing this technique

Power Moves

The power moves are more complex even acrobatic breaking moves that sometimes remind of gymnastics rather than a dance. This technique is very difficult and requires a great deal of speed, momentum, strength, and endurance. The power moves include moves like the windmill, headspin, backspin, or flare. When doing the windmill, breaker spins on the floor, from his back to his chest and back again, and his legs move in the air in a V-shape. There are many starting positions and also many variations of this move. The headspin is a kind of power move in which the dancer rotates on his head often using a cap. During performing this technique is required to be able to keep a perfect balance of the whole body, especially the legs. It is usually performed without any other support, but the use of hands to keep or gain the speed is described as "tapping".

· · ·

F**reeze**

The freeze technique is commonly used to end a power move. It is kind of a pose when the dancer puts his body into a unique position usually holding on his hands and simply stops. There is probably an infinite number of variations of this technique, which is strongly connected to the rhythm of the music. Primarily b-boying took credit for the birth of hip hop because it was the b-boys and b-girls who were the inspiration for DJ Kool Herc in creating the breakbeat. Nevertheless, b-boying or b-girling will probably never be as much important and prominent again as in the era of early hip hop.

Nelson George in Hip Hop America writes that "graffiti has been around since man encountered his first stone wall." It is true that graffiti has been in existence for centuries, but this kind of graffiti has nothing in common with hip hop culture. The style of graffiti that is liked to hip hop was born in Philadelphia the end of the 1960s, where graffiti writers such as Cornbread, Cool Earl and Top Cat had been painting the walls since 1967. This modern graffiti art is also called 'writing' or 'aerosol art'.

The term 'tag' referring to the graffiti is commonly used among graffiti artists and it stands for new names, which artists gave themselves in order to protect them from revelation. A verb 'to tag' was derived from this noun and it means 'to paint' or 'to mark'. The tagging is concerned not only with painting walls, but also buses, trains, subway cars and stations, and many other places in cities. In 1970, a Greek-American teenager started to tag his nickname "TAKI 183" in subway stations of Manhattan because graffiti was so widespread there. In the very same year, the New York Times described "TAKI 183" as the creator of the graffiti phenomenon in New York City.

There are many styles of graffiti around the world. The best-known styles such as tag style, throw-up, wild style, and others will be introduced in the following paragraphs.

Tag style

This style is also called "tagging" and it is the oldest of all graffiti techniques. It is a writer's signature depicted on the streets' walls or in public places to be seen by as many people as possible. To be able to perform this technique one needs just a marker. The main representative of this style was already mentioned TAKI 183. From the beginning, it was just a regular signature, but today, when graffiti is more developed, every writer has its style of writing.

.   .   .

Simple style

It is the basic technique and the first step for a beginning writer. Separately written letters of simple shape are characteristic for this style, in which the basic task is to create one's style and improve one's skills because the letters should have a form of a certain style without any additional elements. This technique is often used by writers when writing a longer text or creating a signature.

Throw-up style

This technique is more advanced than tagging. The throw-ups usually consist of two colors and they are created through the use of spray paint. Throw- up letters have a shape similar to bubbles or even clouds. This technique is often used in "bombing," which means tagging a large number of areas in a night, or when writers want to cover previous works of other artists. The advantage of the throw-up style is that it is very easy and quick to do; it means that it could be done in one stroke and two minutes or less.

· · ·

B**lockbuster style**

The title of this graffiti technique describes the way how letters are written. A blockbuster picture consists of big and square letters and usually of two colors. It is also used to cover earlier works of another artist and this style has the advantage of being easy to write and also easy to read. It is possible to see it on cars, trains, or in places with plenty of space to be able to write the letters nice, big and readable. Because of quite clearly defined square letters, there are not many possibilities how to be creative, and therefore there did not occur any significant changes in this style.

W**ild style**

The wild style is considered to be one of the most difficult techniques. It is a style of complicated, abstract, and very colorful pictures with various additional elements like spikes, arrows and many others. It depends on the writer's own imagination, how the paint will look like. The paintings consist of letters of a certain style, which can drive off in various directions and are connected in some way. It is usually very hard to read paints in this style for the wide public and therefore it is intended especially, but not exclusively, for her graffiti writers, who can without too much trouble decipher these paints based on the connections between letters. Semi-wild style is a kind of wild style graffiti, which is very popular with graffiti writers and the hip hop community. It is very much like wild style, but it is readable and not so time- consuming to paint.

3 **D Style**

The 3D style graffiti is completely different from the other techniques. It is also a very complicated technique with an amazing three-dimensional effect by which shadows play the key role. To be able to do 3D graffiti, a writer needs to know how light and shadows work together. In Martin Fiedler's Hip Hop Forever is stated that "this technique is highly controversial." The problem is that there are writers who think that 3D style is the cream of the graffiti art, and on the other hand, there are writers who do not consider the 3D graffiti artists like writers, but painters. The process of becoming a graffiti writer is difficult and takes a long time. In the beginning, one has to pick a nickname, create one's tag and then it is possible to learn other techniques and develop a personal style. It is also important to learn how to use and apply spray paint and adhere to certain rules concerning graffiti. The process of creating a graffiti painting also is not as easy as it may seem. It includes a lot of effort and imagination of writers, who usually create a sketch before they go tagging. Graffiti is still highly controversial today. On the one hand, a lot of people think that graffiti is just vandalism because it is possible to see a large number of public places that are tagged. On the other hand, there are people who consider graffiti as art and visit galleries and various expositions for that.

5 1990S

In the 80s, hip-hop firmly established itself as both a cultural and commercially viable force; it was still primarily an underground concern. The following decade changed all that. Not only did hip-hop hit arguably its artistic high, but, for the first time, its artists became superstars in their own right. The huge hits of 90s hip-hop put the genre firmly at the top of the heap – a lofty position from which it's never looked back. At the dawn of the 90s, hip-hop faced something of a crisis. The success of gangsta rap groups such as Los Angeles natives NWA, whose 1988 debut album, Straight Outta Compton, detailed street violence in an uncompromising and explicit style, led to many radio stations pulling effective boycotts against hip-hop's more aggressive artists. To make matters worse, Gilbert O'Sullivan's successful court case against Biz Markie, in 1991 (he'd used a sample of O'Sullivan's 'Alone Again (Naturally)' without consent), threatened to change the very way the art form was constructed; no longer could producers use multiple samples, for fear of litigation. On the plus side, artistically, hip-hop was in rude health. The first few years of the decade saw 90s hip-hop classics from the likes of Public Enemy (Fear Of A Black Planet), A Tribe Called Quest (Peoples Instinctive Travels And The Paths Of Rhythm, The Low-End Theory), De La Soul (De La Soul Is Dead) and Main Source (Breaking Atoms). NWA's 1991 follow-up, Efil4zaggin, showed the tables were beginning to turn commercially. The album moved way beyond its urban heartland and into the bedrooms of suburban youth, becoming the first album by a hip-hop group to hit No. 1 on the Billboard 200. By that point, however, the group had started to disintegrate. Ice Cube had left in acrimonious fashion the previous year (releasing his debut solo album, AmeriKKKa's Most Wanted, to critical and commercial success), followed by Dr. Dre, whose own solo career would change the course of hip-hop history.

Forming Death Row Records with Suge Knight and The DOC, Dre used the fledgling imprint to issue his stratospherically popular debut album, The Chronic, at the tail-end of 1992. His revolutionary production style – christened G-Funk – was a canny mix of deep rolling bass, P-Funk-indebted grooves and soulful vocals that smoothed the jagged edges of gangsta rap into a more accessible format which radio stations could get behind. With Death Row Records releasing a succession of hugely successful G-Funk records by artists such as Tha Dogg Pound (Dogg Food) and Snoop Dogg (whose 1993 debut album, Doggystyle, entered the Billboard charts at No.1), 90s hip-hop saw the West Coast usurp its Eastern counterpart as the dominant force in rap music, its artists becoming huge stars and establishing themselves as part of the mainstream.

However, while New York was struggling to compete commercially, its scene was far from stagnant. 1993 saw the release of A Tribe Called Quest's incandescent third album, Midnight Marauders, and the arrival of Wu-Tang Clan, whose groundbreaking debut album, Enter The Wu-Tang: 36 Chambers, heralded a new era for gritty East Coast hip-hop. The following year was just as strong for local talent, with Nas releasing his monumental debut, Illmatic, and Notorious BIG issuing his first, hugely successful, solo venture, Ready To Die. Released on Sean Combs' Bad Boy Entertainment label, that album's hit singles 'Juicy', 'Big Poppa' and 'One More Chance' (which matched Michael Jackson's 'Scream' for the highest-ever debut on the pop charts), led to the album shifting over four million units, turning Biggie into a major star.

The rivalry between the two coasts' hip-hop scenes was, however, far from healthy. In 1995, one of LA's biggest stars, 2Pac, was shot by a pair of muggers while in New York, the day before being found guilty of sexual assault. While in prison, he later accused Sean Combs and former friend Notorious BIG, among others, of being behind the shooting. Suge Knight, who would bail 2Pac out of prison later that year before signing the rapper to Death Row, joined the fray when he publicly insulted Sean Combs on stage at The Source Awards.

2Pac's law-breaking notoriety hadn't done his career any harm, and by the middle of the decade he was not only one of 90s hip-hop's biggest stars, but one of the most bankable acts in music. Released in 1995, while the rapper was still in prison, Me Against The World reached No.1 on the Billboard charts, while the following year he released All Eyez On Me, his first album for Death Row. An astonishing double-album (hip-hop's first) tour de force, All Eyez On Me confirmed 2Pac's status as one of the genre's most singular voices as well as one of its most successful, again hitting No.1, and shifting 566,000 copies in its first week. The simmering feud which had been

building between Death Row and Bad Boy ended trag-
ically. Leaving a Mike Tyson fight in Las Vegas, on 7
September 1996, a car carrying 2Pac and Suge Knight
was peppered with bullets. Six days later, 2Pac died
from his injuries. The following year, Notorious BIG
shared an eerily similar fate after he was shot and
killed in a drive-by shooting. While Biggie's Life After
Death album, released just a few days after, became
the best-selling hip-hop album of all time, the genre
was forced to do some serious soul-searching in its
wake.

Sean Combs was the first to point the route towards a
less opposing fine art. Soon thereafter, like Puff Daddy,
he discharged two benefit singles in memory of his
killed companion. His following hit-laden solo career,
different enterprising interests and prominent relation-
ship with Jennifer Lopez made him a standout amongst
the most conspicuous figures to rise up out of 90s hip-
hop, foretelling another age of rap stars who were as
agreeable on celebrity lane or in the meeting room as
they were in the account studio. Big deal's protégé, Jay
Z, additionally proceeded onward from the clear
brutality of his 1995 debut, Reasonable Doubt. 1997's
In My Lifetime, bridled Sean Combs and Teddy
Riley's radio-accommodating preparations to traverse
into the pop market. Joined with his acclaimed rapping
prowess, the album – and its hit-laden 1998 successor,

Hard Knock Life, slung Jay Z to the genius status he proceeds to hold.

There was one increasingly seismic move in hip-hop before the decade was out. Dr. Dre, who, in 1996, had surrendered Death Row to set up his new steady, Aftermath Entertainment, marked a then little-known Detroit rapper, Eminem, to the name. The following 1999 album, The Marshall Mathers LP, beat the charts. Establishing 90s hip-hop as the point of world-wide strength for the music, the album likewise put Eminem on his way to turning into the top-selling craftsman in music, guaranteeing that hip-hop's very own direction would keep on taking off in the decades that followed. While hip-hop has appreciated various brilliant years, none was as earth-shattering as the 1990s. Rap music both overwhelmed the charts and thrived in the underground, while the establishments for present-day urban music were likewise mapped out. Things could never be the equivalent again. Here are the key factors behind the 1990s case to being the decade in hip-hop history.

NOTORIOUS BIG'S LIFE AFTER DEATH CEMENTS HIS REPUTATION AS THE GREATEST OF ALL TIME

Biggie's gangsta-fied '94 debut, Ready To Die, might have brought East Coast hip-hop back to prominence, but it was its follow-up that confirmed him as an all-time great. Puff Daddy's smooth and soulful productions proved the perfect foil for Biggie's ingenious lyrical turns and charismatic, a smooth-as-silk flow which set a benchmark for MCing that has yet to be bettered. Tragically, it was to prove his swansong. Shot and killed while leaving a party in Los Angeles

JAY Z HONOURS BIGGIE'S LEGACY, PICKS UP THE MANTLE OF GREATEST RAPPER ALIVE WITHIN MY LIFETIME

Hit hard by Biggie's passing, close friend Jay Z toned down the gangsta posturing on his sophomore effort. With Puff Daddy's production team, The Hitmen crafting a pop-leaning, soul-inflected backdrop, Hova delivered a jaw-dropping series of performances that confirmed him as a worthy heir apparent to the throne of the greatest earning rapper. A substantial hit at the time, (the album debuted at No. 3 in the Billboard charts), its savvy mix of tough posturing and pop nous provided the template that would see Jay ultimately become one of the music world's biggest stars.

MISSY ELLIOTT CHARTS HIP-HOP'S FUTURE WITH SUPA DUPA FLY

Refusing to be confined by genre conventions, Missy grabbed hip-hop and R&B by the horns on her debut album. Backed by a youthful Timbaland, whose spare, digital funk and skittery beats added a space-age sheen, Missy's staccato raps, and soulful vocals delivered rhymes that were at once humorous, assertive, intelligent, unique and unforgettable. With Timbaland's productions providing the template for much of the next decade's urban music, Missy forged a revolutionary path for female artists that would be later followed by the likes of Nicky Minaj.

COMPANY FLOW REIGNITE HIP-HOP'S UNDERGROUND WITH FUNCRUSHER PLUS

Despite only releasing one album proper, Company Flow had a stratospheric impact on the hip-hop underground. Angry, defiantly independent

and determined to push rap's envelope with their uncom-
promising approach to production and lyrical flow, they
laid the groundwork for the boldly experimental music
that was to follow in its wake. Co Flow main man El-P is
still going strong with his Run The Jewels project, while
the release also served to put one of the greatest label's in
hip-hop history, Rawkus, on the map. Company Flow
reignites hip-hop's underground with Funcrusher Plus.

SLUM VILLAGE'S DEBUT ALBUM INTRODUCES J DILLA AS HIP-HOP'S GREATEST PRODUCER

While Dilla had been steadily building his
reputation since '95 with stellar productions
for the likes of A Tribe Called Quest, Janet Jackson
and The Pharcyde, it wasn't until he formed Slum
Village, with rappers T3 and Baatin, that the world
was able to enjoy a full album of his warm, soulful and
superlatively percussive productions. Bootlegged at the
time (it wasn't given a full release until years later),
Fan-Tas-Tic has had a lasting impact on a generation of
producers.

WU-TANG CLAN BREAK SALES RECORDS
WITH WU-TANG FOREVER

Any lingering worries record companies may have had about hip-hop's long-term commercial viability must surely have been quelled by the astronomical success of the Wu's sophomore effort. Despite being two hours in length, and prefaced by the similarly unwieldy 'Triumph' single, the Wu's masterplan of releasing multiple solo albums over the previous five years had paid off, as Wu-Tang Forever sold by the bucket-load, becoming the first rap album to debut at Number on both the US and UK mainstream charts

- Ice Cube takes his new crew, Da Lench Mob to New York and records his solo debut with production from The Bomb Squad, Public Enemy's team of producers. The album, "AmeriKKKa's Most Wanted," is praised by the hip-hop community as a classic and sets Cube on the road to solo super stardom.

- Another addition to the (ever-growing) Native Tongues family, Queens-based A Tribe Called Quest to release their debut album, "People's Instinctive Travels and the Paths of Rhythm." Building on the template established by the Jungle Brothers, Queen Latifah, and, most notably, De La Soul; the

group is praised for its intelligently quirky
lyrics and inventive musical style.

- M.C. Hammer continues his pop-rap reign
  with his two Grammy nominations, a new
  Saturday morning cartoon, and an action
  figure. Despite all of his commercial success;
  there is a growing backlash against his image
  and music among rap fans and artists.

- Salt-N-Pepa release their third album, "Blacks
  Magic." The album receives the strongest
  reviews of their career; with the single 'Let's
  Talk About Sex' being especially praised for
  it's honest and thoughtful look at relationships
  and promiscuity.

- After shooting his cousin and leading police
  on a high-speed chase, Slick Rick is captured
  and taken to prison. Def Jam head Russell
  Simmons bails Rick out in time to finish his
  second album, "The Ruler's Back," but Rick is
  eventually sentenced to five years in prison on
  charges of attempted murder

- A video showing four L.A. police officers
  brutally beating a Black man named Rodney

King is played at news stations all over the country. Several rappers contend that this has been happening for years in inner cities and call for change.

- M.C. Hammer releases his third proper album, "2 Legit To Quit." Although the title cut is a sizeable hit; the album fails to match the across-the-board success of its predecessor as the backlash against 'pop-rap' has Hammer losing his (already limited) credibility among rap fans and the general public.

- Dr. Dre; citing a dispute over finances with Eazy-E and Ruthless Records; quits N.W.A. Dre is still under contract to Ruthless; and hires gangster-turned-businessman Marion "Suge" Knight to get him out of his deal with the record label. With Dre departing for a solo career, N.W.A. officially split.

- Sean Combs, still only 20 years old, is promoted to A&R at Uptown Records and executive produces hit albums for Father MC and Heavy D.

- Alternative rap group Main Source release their debut, the critically acclaimed "Breaking Atoms." While it doesn't sell very well, the group becomes among hip-hop's most respected, and the single, 'Live At the Bar-B-Q' features a memorable verse by a seventeen-year-old Queens rapper named Nas.

- 2Pac Shakur, former roadie, dancer, and second-string MC for Digital Underground, releases his debut album, "2Pacalypse Now." It immediately incites controversy for its content; particular lyrics regarding police officers. Vice President Dan Quayle even calls for a ban of the album during his campaign for re-election. Shakur's visibility is also raised by a star-making performance in the gritty urban drama "Juice".

- Body Count; Ice-T's new rap-metal band, release their debut album. The song 'Cop Killa' ignites a fire storm of controversy for it's lyrics about killing police officers. After nationwide protests from law enforcement officials, Time-Warner pressures Ice-T to pull the song from the album and eventually sells its share of Interscope Records, the distributor.

- With "Paul's Boutique" obtaining cult-classic status in the years following it's release; the Beastie Boys third album, "Check Your Head," becomes a smash hit, debuting in the Top Ten and returning the Boys to the charts for the first time since their debut album - although with a much different sound.

- After producing a successful album for R&B singer Mary J. Blige and remixing several other hits for artist such as Jodeci and Heavy D., Sean "Puffy" Combs is fired from Uptown after a dispute with label head Andre Harrell. Snoop Doggy Dogg releases the short film/soundtrack, "Murder Was the Case". With it's graphic storytelling about a man being sentenced for murder uncomfortably close to Snoop's real-life legal woes, many critics blast the rapper for exploiting the unfortunate circumstances.

- "southernplayalisticadillacmuzik," the debut album from Atlanta-based rap duo Outkast signals a shift from hip-hop's bi-coastal grip. Loose and funky with clever lyrics and insightful subject-matter, the group becomes a cult favorite among hip-hop enthusiasts.

• Adding to a seemingly endless string of legal charges, 2Pac is charged with sexual assault by a female fan in New York City.

• Bone Thugs-N-Harmony; a new Cleveland-based rap group discovered by Eazy-E; release an EP called "Creepin' On Ah Come-up." Their sound is a combination of rapid-fire speed-rapping and vocal harmonizing and the single, "Thuggish Ruggish Bone" becomes a moderate hit.

• Notorious B.I.G., after cameo appearances on several popular singles, finally releases "Ready to Die," his debut album for Bad Boy. It spawns two hit singles, 'Juicy' and 'Big Poppa;' one hit remix, 'One More Chance,' and returns the East Coast to the top of the charts after a two-year absence. It also elevates Puffy Combs' Bad Boy label to the top of hip-hop.

- Jay-Z's debut album, "Reasonable Doubt" is released to much praise from critics. Despite all of the accolades, it barely makes a dent on the charts.

- After leaving a Mike Tyson fight in Las Vegas, Nevada; a car carrying Suge Knight and Tupac Shakur is riddled with gunfire. Though Suge only suffers minor injuries, 2Pac--after fighting for his life for seven days in a hospital--dies from his wounds. The hip-hop nation goes into shock and mourning for the fallen rapper.

- Southern rap duo Outkast release their second album, "ATLiens." It is critically acclaimed for its positive outlook, progressive lyrics and a more futuristic production style.

- The Notorious B.I.G. is almost killed in a car accident in New Jersey. With his leg partially shattered, he is forced to walk with a cane. After a year of critical acclaim, The Fugees announce that they are going their separate ways; citing creative differences. Wyclef Jean almost immediately begins work on his solo debut.

- After leaving the Soul Train Music Awards in Los Angeles, the Notorious B.I.G. is shot and killed in a drive-by shooting that eerily resembles what happened to 2 Pac six months earlier. With the twin murders of two of it's biggest stars, the hip-hop nation is forced to take stock of itself and what it represents. B.I.G.'s second album, the prophetically titled "Life After Death," is released only a few days after his killing and becomes the best-selling rap album of all time.

- Sean Combs, now calling himself 'Puff Daddy' releases two benefit singles as memoriam to the slain Notorious B.I.G.

- The Wu-Tang Clan release their second album, the double LP "Wu-Tang Forever." It sells well, but fails to match the critical respect of the group's more acclaimed debut.

- Suge Knight is sentenced to four years in prison for parole violation.

- After writing and producing hits for MC Lyte and R&B groups Xscape and 702; female rap artist Missy "Misdemeanor"

Elliott releases her debut album, "Supa Dupa Fly." It is an artistic triumph and she is praised for her wit and quirky musical approach.

- Puff Daddy makes his debut as an artist with "No Way Out." Spawning four top ten singles, the album becomes a monster hit and makes Puffy the biggest star on the Bad Boy label in the wake of B.I.G.'s murder.

- Snoop Doggy Dogg finally releases his second album, the lackluster "The Doggfather." After the album fails to sell, Snoop announces he is leaving the crumbling Death Row Records.

- After starring in his third-straight summer blockbuster, "Men In Black"; Will Smith confirms his status as one of the biggest box-office draws of the 90s. In a somewhat surprising move, he also returns to music, releasing his first solo album, "Big Willie Style." Though lightweight, it becomes one of the best-selling albums of the year.

- East Coast Queensbridge, NY rappers begin to take over gangsta' rap; led by Nas (Illmatic)

Mobb Deep (Shook Ones) along with Large Professor, Tragedy, Big Noyd and others from the Borough

- Ending a five-year period of seclusion that saw his reputation as a lyricist reach near-mythic proportions; Rakim finally makes his return with "The 18th Letter," his solo debut.

- Def Squad dominates after EPMD's split. Redman, K-Solo, Jamal, Keith Murray takes over and their hits filled ears worldwide

- After operating in obscurity in the Deep South for almost a decade, New Orleans based rapper-entrepreneur Master P releases "Ghetto D." Derided by critics as an untalented hack; the album nonetheless becomes a hit and opens the floodgates for a wealth of New Orleans gangsta rap to hit the airwaves. Master P, as founder and CEO of the No Limit record label, unexpectedly becomes one of the most powerful men in hip-hop.

- Picking up where the Notorious B.I.G. left off (at least commercially), new Bad Boy rapper

Ma$e releases his debut album, "Harlem World." It is a smash and confirms Bad Boy's status as the (now undisputed) top label in rap.

- Def Jam Records signs Jay-Z and releases popular albums by rappers Redman, Method Man, and Foxy Brown; signalling a return to form for Russell Simmons and rap's longest-running label.

- Simmons also signs a newly-reformed EPMD and DMX, an intense MC from Yonkers. Jay-Z releases his second album, "In My Lifetime." It sells much better than his debut, but critics deride it as a flaky attempt to reach a crossover audience.

- Afeni Shakur, mother of the slain 2Pac Shakur; releases "R U Still Down (Remember Me)," a double-album of unreleased material the rapper recorded before his death. It is the beginning of a flood of songs, compilations and albums from the deceased rap star's vaults.

- DMX makes his debut with "It's Dark and Hell Is Hot" and intensely personal album of hard-core rap and poignant confessionals. It becomes a monster hit and signals a return of gritty, hard-core rap after a year of the more radio-friendly, Bad Boy-influenced party-rap.

- Master P's No Limit Records continues to churn out one hit album after the other; even though critics and hip-hop purists scoff at the cheap production and lackluster artists on the label. Seeking to strike while he's hot, P also creates No Limit Films, No Limit Wireless, and his own Percy Miller Clothing Line.

- Jay-Z's third album,: Hard Knock Life," becomes his biggest-seller and restores some of his credibility in hip-hop circles. He immediately is heralded as the biggest rapper in hip-hop.

- Lauryn Hill, formerly of the Fugees; releases her solo debut, "The Miseducation of Lauryn Hill." With an emphasis on confessional songwriting and a powerful mix of rap, reggae, gospel, soul and folk, it becomes the most-acclaimed album of the year and thrusts Hill into international stardom.

- "Aquemini;" the third outing for Atlanta rappers Outkast; is a startling leap forward for the group. Combining live instruments with thought-provoking and forward-thinking lyrics, as well as meshing hip-hop, country, soul, techno, and funk elements, the album follows Lauryn Hill's debut as one of the most acclaimed albums of the year, though it isn't as successful commercially.

- Camp Lo dropped their Coolie High, Luchini and then released their first album, Uptown Saturday Night which put the fashioned-desi rappers on scene, incomparable to none.

- After releasing their fifth album, "The Love Movement," A Tribe Called Quest abruptly announce their breakup. Lead rapper Q-Tip immediately embarks on a solo career.

- Seeking a career rebirth, Snoop Dogg signs with Master P's No Limit label and rush-releases two lackluster albums.

- With a chain of restaurants, ("Justin's"), a clothing line, ("Sean John"), and a celebrity girlfriend, (Jennifer Lopez), Puff Daddy becomes the most recognized producer in hip-hop.

Hip-hop music is the vehicle of hip-hop culture and contains "rapping" (superimposed with vocals) by emcees. Inferable from this, hip-hop music is sometime alluded to as "rap music," However, the individuals who reject hip-hop as rap music don't fathom its rich history and the impact this classification of music has on youth.

Hip-hop music is a vehicle utilized by artists to address bigotry, mistreatment, and neediness issues. It describes stories of inward city African-Americans living the American dream from the base up, and harshly addresses racial segregation, broken homes, and conquering misfortune. Created by Jamaican vagrant DJ Kool Herc in the mid-70s in New York City, it has from that point forward spread its appendages over the world. Herc moved from reggae records to funk, shake and disco. Inferable from the short percussive breaks, he started broadening them utilizing a sound blender and two records.

As the remarkable style of music turned into a hit, performers (emcees) started superimposing the music with vocals; at first, they presented themselves as well as other people in the group of spectators. Afterward, the rapping turned out to be progressively differing, fusing brief rhymes, frequently with a sexual or brutal subject, trying to engage the group of spectators.

In the mid-1970s, hip-hop split into two gatherings. One concentrated on getting the group moving, another featured rapid-fire rhymes.

The 1980s saw a further enhancement in hip-hop; very figurative lyrics rapping over multi-layered beats supplanted basic vocals. During the 90s, gangsta rap (celebrated bandit way of life) moved toward becoming standard. Hip-hop was soon a necessary part of standard music, and about all the pop melodies highlighted a hidden component of hip-hop.

During the 90s and into the next decade, components of hip-hop were coordinated into differing classes of music: hip-hop soul joined hip-hop and soul music; in the Dominican Republic, an account by Santi Y Sus Duendes and Lisa M was begotten "Meren-rap," a combination of hip-hop and meringue. In Europe, Africa, and Asia, hip-hop has experienced progress from an underground event to the standard market.

Hip Hop gives point by point information on Hip Hop, Hip Hop And Rap, Hip Hop Music, R&B Hip Hop and these are just the beginning. Hip Hop affiliated with Karaoke Music Hip-hop is something other than music. The term incorporates an entire culture, and that clarifies how it has turned out to be a standout amongst the most compelling components molding global entertainment and youth self-expression. Everywhere throughout the world hip-hop is a device for clarifying the complexities of day by day life and speaking truth to control, whether through spoken lyrics, graffiti, art, dance or circle racer dominance. Not to be mistaken for business rap which frequently praises material overabundance, brutality, and misogyny—hip-hop was conceived in the South Bronx, New York, more than 40 years prior as an option in contrast to reckless pack culture. Hip-hop gave offended youth in devastated neighborhoods a chance to channel their dissatisfactions into art as opposed to brutality.

Hip hop music is part of hip hop culture predominately among African Americans and Latinos (the other two components are spray painting art and breakdancing). The explanations behind the ascent in hip hop music are found in the changing urban culture in the United States in the 1970s. Starting in the 1980s, hip hop culture started its spread over the world. By setting aside the effort to clarify a ripe culture articulation, understudies of hip hop music place available to us the absolute most interesting examinations of a ground-breaking art form. More than a musical style, hip-hop is a past filled with American culture and a declaration by its artists of their background. In 1985, when Run-DMC appointed themselves the "Lords of Rock," in the lyrics of their hit melody of a similar name, they likely never envisioned that one day they would be perceived all things considered. As the pioneers of hip-hop music, they persuaded the world to dance to verse with a beatbox. They welcomed any individual who might tune in to "Walk This Way" in "My Adidas," right to the highest priority on VH1's rundown of the 50 Greatest Hip-Hop Artists.

The lyrics found in hip hop music are articulations that are connected with social and societal sentiments of a person. Hip hop lyrics are known for their conversational quality. Hip hop lyrics are utilized to show expressive highlights, symbolism, sound similarity, similar sounding word usage, cadenced structure, and rhyme are educated while essential proficiency (vowels, consonants, mixes, syllables, and spelling) is implanted.

Hip hop lyrics ordinarily utilize internal city slang with lovely gadgets, for example, similar sounding word usage, sound similarity, and rhyme. The slang of hip hop lyrics may incorporate words like, yo, dis, stream, phat and homie. Hip hop lyrics have been compared to what shake music lyrics used to be, and sometimes have replaced shake and society melodies inside the culture. Hip hop lyrics contain numerous references that the audience members can identify with. Hip hop lyrics that recount overabundance riches and extravagance of artists may interface with a gathering of people with such dreams. As in the language, hip hop lyrics are verse, however, verse with something more added to it. Some hip hop lyrics are incredibly articulate in that they express a specific subject in an alternate form. Even though the facts confirm that numerous hip hop lyrics are slang it is likewise evident that quite a bit of our normal spoken language is slang and once in a while profane. Subsequently, enabling us to see that there is a contrast among distinct and prescriptive language. Adding to the hip hop music and tune lyrics, moving is another component of the hip hop culture otherwise called the hip hop dance style. Hip hop dance is a collective development that consistently develops and advances through individual spontaneous creation. Hip hop dance is an art form that has the country and world attempting to one-two stage or breakdance to krumping.

Hip hop music and moving, or breaking, ascended in the 1970s and 1980s, fixated on urban networks of youthful dancers and musicians and their pop culture. Hip hop moving keeps on developing into various forms today, intensely impacted by the advancement of music and its fame in the media. Hip-hop is a strenuous dance style that includes utilizing the whole body to make sharp, expressive developments. As in all dance forms, hip hop dance is a system with characterized steps and developments that must be learned and rehearsed.

Hip hop music is a famous style of music. It is wherever from plugs to TV sitcoms. Hip hop culture and music go from those much the same as standard prevalent music to the blues form of the human condition. There is a major impact of R&B in the hip hop music industry that gives a thrilling knowledge to the audience. This urban culture is clearing the world in music, motion pictures, and clubs. It is an American minority creation which merits more acknowledge and acknowledgment as an art form as opposed to as a trend which should simply blur away with time.

8 HIP HOP AND THE YOUTH

Violence in rap isn't full of a feeling operator that takes steps to hurt America's youth; rather, it is the objection of an effectively existing issue from youth whose world views have been formed by encountering profound economic disparities separated to a great extent along racial lines. The agnostic way to deal with violence and crime for which rap is regularly censured is protected by certain craftsmen as the reasonable aftereffect of the variations that face African-American communities, from which rap began and remained established.

America's latest enumeration announced that African-American youth are the in all likelihood bunch in the country to live in poor family units and neighborhoods, to be jobless, to be the casualties of manslaughter or AIDS, or to invest energy in jail sooner or later in their lifetimes. For some poor, inward city youth, the weapon, which has had a focal job in the verses of numerous gangsta rappers, speaks to an approach to enable oneself and increase regard inside proceeding with cycles of racial and economic preference. More-over, a few rappers protect the nearness of violence in their verses as the manifestation of American history and culture. By indicating rap as the reason for violence, government officials endeavor to eradicate from the cognizance of their constituents the historical backdrop of abuse that has brought forth hip-hop culture.

In request to really change the approaching nearness of violence in American society, as symptomized by violence in motion pictures, television, and music, the rest of the issues of destitution and bias in America's urban communities must be forcefully tended to. Amusingly, huge numbers of similar legislators and gatherings who shout out against violence in rap music are additionally driving the assault on Welfare, Affir-mative Action, subsidizing for instruction, and recom-mendations for all-inclusive medicinal services. It is inconsistencies in financial and political power, not hip-hop music, that make violence in American soci-ety. Cutting programs that provide social administra-tions to help reduce the unequal opportunity to employment, assets, and social versatility will just serve to exasperate issues. Voters must not enable themselves to be tricked into accepting that censorship can safe-monitor kids from the repercussions of violence in American culture; they should not play into the issue by cutting programs that provide hope for departure from financial and political disparities that feed into the cycle of violence. Instead, the individuals who wish to put a conclusion to the issues communicated by certain rappers in their verses and ways of life must concentrate on giving administrations and openings that will battle the sentiment of agnosticism in a significant number of America's people group today. Social administrations must be upheld, extended, and redesigned to all the more successfully oversee programs for the individuals who have been financially and politically distraught. It is important to address the essential needs of the regular urban workers - moderate lodging, human services, and sustenance - before there can be any endeavors to take out violence in America's urban areas.

Furthermore, it is essential that regular workers grown-ups can gain a living compensation before they may start to be required to have hope for their future or the fate of their youngsters. The lowest pay permitted by law, as it exists today, isn't a sufficient family wage, and, subsequently, numerous guardians have been compelled to maintain a few sources of income, fending off them from home, to provide for their kids and relatives. At last, to forestall violence and wrong-doing before it starts, government, state, and nearby financing ought to be occupied from law authorization and jail frameworks into government funded training and youth programs. Youth can't have hope except if they approach a helpful, important instruction that can provide them with the opportunity to pick the way of their fates. I accept that couple of youth, given adequate assets, regard, and backing would pick violence. In any case, for some youth today, alternatives are constrained by a difference of access to the assets that provide that decision.

For some youth, the legends and success accounts of the inward city are rappers. The prevalence of rap and the turn off of hip-hop culture- - style lines like FUBU and Tommy Hilfiger, motion pictures, for example, Boyz N Da Hood and Friday, and television shows like The Fresh Prince of Bel-Air and In the House- - have majorly affected American promoting patterns.

The intrigue of hip-hop culture has pushed out of urban territories and into suburbia. Hip-hop has affected standard design, television, films, publicizing, and language Hoping to pursue the success of rappers like LL Cool J, Will Smith, Sean "Puffy" Combs, and Wyclef, numerous youth consider them to be industry as one of their solitary chances to accomplish the repu-tation and cash to get away from the hopelessness of the internal city. Nonetheless, the individuals who endeavor to prevail in hip-hop music face a trouble-some test. In an industry constrained by for the most part by high society white men, youthful, urban minority musicians are frequently treated as products, not as specialists. They should adjust a requirement for aesthetic control and "keepin' it real" with the confine-ments and weights from record organizations keen on producing deals and huge intrigue. Regularly the message and imaginative respectability of rappers can be lost in the midst of national showcasing efforts and worry for endorsement by significant business partners, for example, Wal-Mart and MTV.

In the developing success of the hip-hop showcase, musicians have attempted to keep up rap's intensity as a form of opposition and strengthening. To safeguard rap's social capacity and, all the while, to advance masterful and business advance, the networks that have generally been the ones making the music ought to be the ones that control its generation and dispersion.

Hip-hop must be perceived as a musical form and not just a business pattern. Hip-hop, including its history, its forms, and its social significance, ought to be educated in school music education programs close by traditional music, people music, and jazz. The incorporation of rap in music instruction programs may likewise enable understudies and instructors to have open discussions on related issues, for example, the relationship among rap and posses, the nearness of violence, misogyny, and homophobia in some rap tunes, and the discussion over musical rating and warning frameworks.

Hip-hop ought to be grasped in state-funded school music programs as an American development and an approach to relate understudy interests with educational modules. Moreover, rap could be coordinated into English and language expressions educational modules as a form of both verse and show. Enabling understudies to compose and perform their own rap urges them to think basically, to work on writing in the account form, to build vocabulary, and to build up a comprehension of rhyme and musicality. Internal city youth associations, for example, the Boys and Girls Club or the YMCA, can execute programs that advance enthusiasm for hip-hop music. These associations give youth the order, self-assurance, leadership, and different instruments essential for success in the music industry. They might most likely work with nearby radio and television stations and record marks - particularly those began and claimed by African-

Americans, for example, Def Jam and Bad Boy- - to provide open doors for internships, visits, and employment shadow days that give youth involvement in the music industry. They may enable youth to sort out, advance, and perform in hip-hop shows held routinely at the club. Including youth at all dimensions of arranging provides an important experience that engages them in the music industry and different aspects of the business.

Eventually, by enabling youth to see and experience how hip-hop is formed, contrarily and decidedly, by the matter of the music industry, they have the learning to settle on informed musical choices and, potentially, to make a change in the activities of the music industry.

9 CULTURE OF HIP HOP AND
SOCIAL CONSCIOUSNESS

As of late, debate encompassing rap music has been in the cutting edge of the American media. From the promotion of the East Coast-West Coast contention that shadowed the killings of rappers Tupac Shakur and Notorious B.I.G. to the vilification of modem music in the wake of acts of mass violence in Littleton, Colorado, it appears that political and media gatherings have rushed to place fault on rap for an appearing pattern in youth brutality.

In any case, however pundits rush to call attention to the rough verses of certain rappers; they are over-looking what's important of rap's message.

Rap, as different types of music, can't be compre-hended except if it is contemplated without the edge of its recorded and social setting. The present rap music mirrors its starting point in the hip-hop culture of youthful, urban, average workers African-Americans, its foundations in the African oral custom, its capacity as the voice of a generally underrepresented gathering, and, as its notoriety has developed, its commercializa-tion and assignment by the music industry. Hip-hop music is commonly considered to have been spear-headed in New York's South Bronx in 1973 by Jamaican-conceived Kool DJ Herc. At a Halloween dance gathering tossed by his more youthful sister, Herc utilized an inventive turntable system to extend a song's drum break by playing the break segment of two indistinguishable records continuously. The fame of the all-encompassing break loaned its name to "break-dancing"- - a style explicit to hip-hop culture, which was encouraged by expanded drum breaks played by DJs at New York dance parties. By the mid-1970s, New York's hip-hop scene was ruled by original turntablists, DJ Grandmaster Flash, Afrika Bambaataa, and Herc. The rappers of Sugarhill Gang created hip-hop's first industrially effective hit, "Rapper's Delight," in 1979'.

Rap itself- - the rhymes expressed over hip-hop music- - started as an editorial on the capacity or abilities of a specific DJ while that DJ was playing records at a hip-hop occasion. MCs, the precursors of the present rap artists, presented DJs and their songs and frequently perceived the nearness of companions in the crowd at hip-hop exhibitions. Their job was cut out by well known African-American radio plate maneuvers in New York during the late 1960s, who presented songs and artists with unconstrained rhymes. The development of MCs grabbed the eye of hip-hop fans. Their rhymes lapped over from the change time frame between the finish of one song and the acquaintance of the following with the songs themselves. Their analyses moved exclusively from a DJ's abilities to their very own encounters and stories. The job of MCs in exhibitions climbed relentlessly, and they started to be perceived as artists in their very own right. The neighborhood prevalence of the cadenced music served by DJs at dance parties and clubs joined with an expansion in 'b-young men'- breakdancers and spray painting artists and the developing significance of MCs made a particular culture known as hip-hop.

Generally, hip-hop culture was characterized and grasped by youthful, urban, common laborers African-Americans. Hip-hop music started from a mix of generally African-American types of music-- including jazz, soul, gospel, and reggae. It was made by regular workers African-Americans, who, like Herc, exploited accessible apparatuses - vinyl records and turntables-- to develop another type of music that both communicated and molded the culture of dark New York City youth during the 1970s.

While rap's history seems brief its connection to the African oral tradition, which furnishes rap with quite a bit of its present social importance, likewise roots rap in a long-standing history of oral students of history, melodious fetishism, and political promotion. At the core of the African oral tradition is the West African3 thought of nommo. In Malian Dogon cosmology, Nommo is the main human, a making of the incomparable divinity, Amma, whose imaginative power lies in the generative property of the spoken word4. As a philosophical idea, nommo is the animative capacity of words and the conveyance of words to follow up on items, giving life. The centrality of nommo in the African oral tradition has offered the capacity to rappers and rap music inside numerous African-American communities.

Rap's normal assignment as "CNN for dark individuals" may result from the descendence of rappers from griots, regarded African oral history specialists and acclaim vocalists. Griots were the guardians and purveyors of information, including innate history, family heredity, and updates on births, passings, and wars. Voyaging griots spread learning in an available form- - the verbally expressed word- - to individuals from ancestral towns. So also, in the United States, numerous rappers make songs that, through performances and records, spread updates on their day by day lives, dreams, and discontents outside of their prompt neighborhoods.

Rappers are seen as the voice of poor, urban African-American youth, whose lives are commonly rejected or distorted by the predominant press. They are the attendants of contemporary African-American average workers history and concerns. Furthermore, rap's potential for political support comes from the capacity of its antecedents, African-American rhyming diversions, as forms of protection from frameworks of enslavement and servitude. Rhyming games encoded race relations between African-American slaves and their white experts in a manner that enabled them to pass the investigation of suspicious managers. Furthermore, rhyming diversions enabled captives to utilize their inventive mind to give motivation and stimulation. For instance, by describing the slave as a bunny and the ace as a fox, "Brer Rabbit stories" camouflaged accounts of slaves outmaneuvering their lords and getting away ranches behind the veneer of a funny experience.

Hip-hop writer, Davey D associates the African oral tradition to present day rap: "You see, the slaves were brilliant and they talked in similitudes. They would be executed if the slave bosses heard them talking in new tongues. So they did what advanced rappers do- - they flexed their melodious skillz."

Rap has created as a form of protection from the oppression of common laborers African-Americans in urban focuses. Despite the fact that it might be seen essentially as a form of amusement, rap has the ground-breaking potential to address social, economic, and political issues and go about as a bringing together voice for its group of spectators. Rap imparts its under-lying foundations to different forms of traditionally African-American music, for example, jazz, blues, and soul. Rap may likewise be firmly connected to reggae music, a sort that additionally created from the blend of traditional African drumming and the music of the European decision class by the youth of constrained economic methods inside an arrangement of African economic oppression. In an amusing circle of impact,

Jamaican reggae was played on African-American radio stations in New York during the 1960s. DJs utilized rhymes to present reggae songs. These stations could be gotten in Jamaica, where audience members grabbed on the DJs' rhyming styles, extending them over reggae songs to make "name"- - another precursor of rap.

Kool DJ Herc, before presenting his creative turntable style, brought his name style to New York, yet it neglected to pick up notoriety. He focused on building up his DJing abilities, which later took into consideration the acknowledgment of MCing and, in the long run, rap.

The advancement of rap and reggae has been an interlaced way of two distinct styles, which have developed from and have flourished, in comparative conditions. At long last, similarly, as reggae has been enduring an onslaught for certain craftsmen's appearing promotion of violence to unravel social, political, and economic issues, rap has turned into the substitute of the American musical texture, as it, as well, has confronted mass prevalence and commercialization. Similarly, as reggae is currently under danger of losing its capacity as a work of art and a social voice" in the wake of being appropriated by those outside of the Rastafarian culture, rap battles to endure reception and commodification by that outside of the universe of hip-hop.

In recent decades, hip-hop music has pursued the way of commercialization that wrecked African-American radio stations in the 1970s. Though preceding commercialization, African-American proprietors, software engineers, and DJs had the opportunity to utilize their stations to serve the particular needs of their audience members - New York's average worker's African-American community. They had the option to advance nearby craftsmen and occasions and to address news occasions and social worries as individuals from a similar community from which they drew their group of spectators. Nonetheless, as enterprises claimed by businessmen outside of the community united power by buying nearby stations, African-American AM stations were constrained out of the market by more economically-ground-breaking stations possessed and controlled principally by individuals from the white high society. African - American DJs lost their influence as the cutting edge griots of their communities and as the moderators of hip-hop music and culture. Similarly, with the revelation of hip-hop craftsmen by corporate record names, rap music was stolen from its community, repackaged by cash disapproved of businessmen hoping to make a more extensive intrigue by eradicating hip-hop's memorable capacity, and sold back to the avenues through showcasing ploys, for example, music recordings and Top-40 outlines.

By the 1980s, hip-hop had turned into a business and rap music was an important product and rap's commodification has likewise disappointed it as a form of obstruction. Corporate America's fixation on rap has expanded as the class' political substance has wilted. Ice Cube's initial songs assaulted white bigotry; Ice-T sang a song about a cop executioner; Public Enemy moved audience members to "fight the power." In any case, numerous more up to date acts are centered on the whole around pathologies inside the black community. They now rap about shooting different blacks, yet never about testing legislative expert or empowering social activism. In spite of the fact that not new topics, huge numbers of the parts of rap that have been brought up by government officials as "frightful"- - violence, misogyny, and homophobia in the verses and ways of life of certain rappers- - might be viewed as a component of rap's commodification. While rappers battle to "keep it real"- - a term which reminds those inside hip-hop to be consistent with their underlying foundations - some concede that numerous rappers do as their record marks wish- - just, they compose verses that are permitted. In a group of people which has moved toward becoming progressively ethnically and economically   different,   business-disapproved   of rappers have been compelled to take on the restricted jobs that have demonstrated beneficial for youthful; African-American male specialists - that of the "pimp," the "gangsta", and the "playa." The commodification of rap has permitted huge checks and platinum records to eradicate the verifiable, social, and economic settings, out of which rap has developed, from open cognizance. As indicated by Davey D, "The matter of music has degraded rap." from its foundations as opposition against servitude to its association with the reggae development in Jamaica to the presence of rappers as cutting edge griots, rap has traditionally been the music of the enslaved African-American common laborers.

While it is critical to commend hip-hop culture today as comprehensive of incomprehensibly different ethnic and economic gatherings, it is similarly imperative to perceive and protect the capacity that rap has served for its unique community. So as to comprehend the subjects and forms of rap music, it is essential to pursue the history of African-Americans from their beginnings in West Africa, to their subjugation all through the early history of the United States, to their battles against racial preference and isolation after Emancipation, to the proceeding with fights against true economic isolation and recovery of social personality of numerous African-Americans today. In the event that rap music gives off an impression of being too much rough when contrasted with nation western or mainstream shake, it is on the grounds that rap comes from a culture that has been leaked in the battle against political, social, and economic persecution. Notwithstanding the showy behavior now and then put on for real mark collections or MTV videos, for some, specialists, rapping about guns and drug life is an impression of day by day life in racially-and economically-stratified internal city ghettos and lodging ventures.

UNIFICATION AND EDUCATION

One of these positive impacts is that it has been used as an incredible unifier of various populaces around the globe. It began as a subculture among African American communities in America yet it is presently a wonder of worldwide culture. In actuality, it isn't just confined to African American communities, as communities of color contain seventy-five percent of the worldwide hip hop group of spectators. The way that hip hop has crossed the social separation exhibits its capacity to bring together a large number of youth around the world. This is reminiscent of when shake music was on everybody's lips universally. The development of hip hop culture is conspicuous in the urban road style of

dressing duplicated from hip hop artists. The trade-
mark highlights of this style are loose jeans, tops worn
in reverse just as costly tennis shoes, which gives young
people a feeling of character. Hip hop has been crucial
in advancing social and political mindfulness among
the youth of today. Hip hop music teaches individuals
from a few alternate points of view and raises
numerous social issues. Hip hop is a channel for indi-
viduals to talk unreservedly about their view on polit-
ical or social issues and like this, it draws in youngsters
to wind up concerned and mindful of these issues.
This is significant in making the youth mindful of their
general surroundings and the conditions they face in
the public eye, empowering people to talk about
manners by which they can roll out a positive improve-
ment inside society. A couple of the issues that hip hop
has made mindfulness in racial separation, distinction
and the significance of training and putting stock in
your fantasies. Hip hop additionally is an impression of
the spirit and mind and is a comfort for both the artists
and audience members who might battle with similar
issues. Music, as a rule, unites individuals, however,
the youth of today can identify with the battle and
challenges that most rappers talk about. Since the
arrival of Grandmaster Flash's "The Message" in 1982,
hip hop music has received an increasingly political
tone. Hip hop music, more than some other classifica-

tion, has cautioned both private and open residents of the predicament of the lower classes in urban zones among different issues. Some hip-hoppers are known for their dubious verses can frequently point out more noteworthy issues.

HOPE

Many rappers rap about destitution and their battles in inward city America while growing up. When they make progress, they talk about conquering hindrances and ascending to the top. This message can give hope to numerous youths crosswise over America who live in comparable conditions. For instance, when a rapper raps about his tested youth or about prevailing regardless of living with a medication dependent parent, an adolescent in a comparable circumstance may accept that he, as well, can get past his battles.

SOCIAL AWARENESS

Through training and understanding, hip hop music has impelled social mindfulness in communities around the nation. Hip hop music has filled in as an apparatus to stand in opposition to negative parts of life, for example, brutality and firearms. Numerous artists use their musical abilities to advance harmony and hostile to rough acts. By imparting messages about brutality and separation, and identifying with youth individuals, it gives a chance to them to roll out positive improvements in their own life. Rappers, for example, the late Tupac Shakur were frequently reprimanded for their verses, which illustrated urban America. While such verses were maybe somewhat expected to stun buyers, they additionally carried attention to the nation's social problems, especially those in the inward city. Issues, for example, viciousness, illicit drug use, and destitution are on the whole normal topics in hip hop music. When somebody tunes in to the class, he might do as such for stimulation, however, he won't most likely abstain from finding out about these issues and offering thought to them. There is some hip hop music that is made with the expectation of sending a positive message to its group of spectators. There are melodies that reprove viciousness and call for more harmony and fellowship in the inward city trying to improve personal satisfaction. One incredible case of a rap melody that sends this message is entitled "Implosion" and performed by the East Coast All Stars. Presently for you Hip-Hop students of history, I realize this returns a long while, however it is a standout amongst the best instances of the positive impact of hip hop music. A gathering of free rap artists got together to make this tune because they knew about the extraordinary power and impact that they have with their music and were endeavoring to use that impact to roll out a positive improvement. This venture filled two significant needs because it didn't just make consciousness of the internal city's problems with viciousness, however, it additionally demonstrated that rappers could be socially cognizant and make music that was positive.

OFFERING HELP

When managing social problems, a standout amongst the most significant methods for finding an answer for the issue is to make others inside our general public mindful of it. Hip hop music is an incredible instrument for encouraging that procedure because of its fame; it can carry a message to the majority. By far, most of the rap artists are from inner cities where below average social conditions and imbalance can be seen the most. Ordinarily, when a rapper composes a melody that discusses savagery, sedate use or other criminal activity, it is because it is something that they have found in their living condition and this manner are in a decent position to give a point by point record of how life is there. A few rappers may confess to taking an interest in a portion of the previously mentioned activity however once more, isn't constantly imply that they are commending it. A specific story might be advised to give hope and let an audience realize that because they have committed errors previously, it doesn't imply that they can't change their life and be engaged with something positive. The rappers use their music to bring issues to light of these issues with the goal that some center can be put into improving them.

ENTERTAINMENT

Hip hop music's universally useful is to engage its crowd. Because a rapper paints themselves in an image of being related in criminal activity, burning through a large number of dollars on apparently pointless things or having intercourse with different ladies doesn't imply that they really do. On numerous events, the rap craftsman is making a fictionalized record of specific occasions for the reason for charming and engaging individuals and now and again uses characters to encourage those records. A portion of the more capable rappers can use their words to make these characters alongside striking storylines that frequently are identified with an urban topic. This is the same as different types of stimulation, specifically, the film business. When we watch our preferred on-screen character conveying and utilizing their firearms to slaughter individuals, devouring medications, or being depicted exceedingly explicitly in a film, it isn't viewed as a ruffian. A portion of the characters being made in these motion pictures is the same than a portion of the characters that are made in hip hop music. Because a rapper says that they do certain things in their music, it doesn't imply that they generally do. While the pictures that are displayed in some rap music can surely be viewed as an awful impact, it doesn't imply that all hip hop music is degenerate. Is it degenerate when holy places use Christian rap in their administration to communicate something specific? Is it degenerate when cops, firemen, and instructors use it to spread their message and endeavor to make an association with the youth?

PROGRAMS

Rap music is an extraordinary and incredible asset that can be used for good purposes. When evaluating rap music, one needs to go past the outside of what they are hearing and endeavor to learn the message that the music is endeavoring to send. Projects Rap and hip hop are being used inside the social work field as a type of therapy. Hip-Hop Therapy uses hip hop culture and music to draw in youth and address their issues in therapy. The objective is to get youth patients to think about their past encounters by interfacing with hip hop lyrics. Recently grassroots associations have jumped up in the United States that plan to use hip hop and rap to diminish youth savagery. In Tucson, Arizona, Usiel Barrios has made basic Hip Hop Skool, which plans to use hip hop to get youngsters engaged with network building. This program intends to engage youngsters with leadership abilities, support positive self-articulation, and advance network contribution – through hip hop. Another grassroots association that has been made as of late is, Project Spitfire. This association was established by Henry Mann and means to combine youthful musicians with expert makers who help them record melodies and recordings. Firecracker additionally gives artists a $100 marking reward, photography shoots, and exposure. Firecracker expects to sign youthful artists who talk about change and options. They will likely sign artists who can show the youth that there are options in contrast to packs and savagery. Mann needs to give youthful rappers a road to recount to their accounts and past lived encounters in the hope that it will impact change in the youth culture.

AFTERWORD

Hip Hop has moved past it humble beginnings in the South Bronx and all through street corners and arranged spaces in American culture and culture. It has moved from negligible verses and basement parties to issues in presidential discussions and sentiments, just as, in each dimension of the legal executive. It is the subject matter of children's' storybooks to all things considered for doctorates. Hip Hop holdings and accumulations are in exhibition halls at Harvard University to pretty much every community library in the country.

The culture of Hip Hop is as yet alive on the streets and in tha' 'hood as much for what it's worth in the institute. From its refusal to being on MTV to getting to be one of the biggest broad communications and promoting 'item,' hip hop is solid and frail in various ways. It is implanted in American culture on all coasts and from mean-street to fundamental street. As much as it is grounded, it is extraterrestrial - compliments of NASA.

Hip Hop as a worldwide wonder is verifiable, and as a social and corporate power, it is a seething bull. It is one of the major sociological occasions and subjects of this modern era and it merits expanding consideration in the speculations and investigations of the sociologies and humanities. Its traces have expanded as the writings have created.

Hip Hop is absolutely not traditional but rather a missional emanation of having a contract for the cultures of the seized. It's a human science as much as a sociological viewpoint on urban culture.